COLLEGE OF ALAMEDA L

WITHDRAWN

LENDING POLICY:
IF YOU DAMAGE OR LOSE LIBRARY MATERIALS,
YOU WILL BE CHARGED FOR REPLACEMENT.
FAILURE TO PAY AFFECTS LIBRARY PRIVILEGES
GRADES, TRANSCRIPTS, DIPLOMAS, AND REGISTRATION
PRIVILEGES OR ANY COMBINATION THEROF.

D0516564

Smithsonian

Goes Wild

Goes

Amy Pastan and Linda McKnight

Smithsonian

Wild

Collins

An Imprint of HarperCollinsPublishers

SMITHSONIAN GOES WILD. Copyright © 2007 by Amy Pastan and McKnight Design, LLC.
All rights reserved. Printed in China. No part of this book may be used or reproduced in any manner whatsoever without written permission except in the case of brief quotations embodied in critical articles and reviews. For information, address HarperCollins Publishers, 10 East 53rd Street, New York, NY 10022.

HarperCollins books may be purchased for educational, business, or sales promotional use. For information please write: Special Markets Department, HarperCollins Publishers, 10 East 53rd Street, New York, NY 10022.

FIRST EDITION

All images © Smithsonian Institution, except as noted.
The name of the "Smithsonian," "Smithsonian Institution," and the sunburst logo are registered trademarks of the Smithsonian Institution.

Designed by Linda McKnight, McKnight Design, LLC
Edited by Anita Schwartz
The authors would like to thank Ellen Nanney of Smithsonian Business Ventures for coordinating this project. Her efforts made this book series possible.

Library of Congress Cataloging-in-Publication Data
Pastan, Amy.
    Smithsonian goes wild / Amy Pastan and Linda McKnight. — 1st ed.
        p. cm.
    ISBN 978-0-06-125149-8
1. Felidae—Exhibitions. 2. Smithsonian Institution—Exhibitions. I.
McKnight, Linda, 1947- II. Title.

QL737.C23P363 2007
599.75074'753—dc22   2007018348

07 08 09 10 11   TP   10 9 8 7 6 5 4 3 2 1

The authors would like to thank the following Smithsonian museums, research centers, and offices for their assistance and cooperation in the making of Spotlight Smithsonian books:

Anacostia Community Museum
Archives of American Art
Arthur M. Sackler Gallery
Cooper-Hewitt, National Design Museum
Freer Gallery of Art
Hirshhorn Museum and Sculpture Garden
National Air and Space Museum
National Air and Space Museum's
    Steven F. Udvar-Hazy Center
National Anthropology Archives
National Museum of African Art
National Museum of American History,
    Kenneth E. Behring Center
National Museum of the American Indian
National Museum of Natural History
National Portrait Gallery
National Postal Museum
National Zoological Park
Smithsonian American Art Museum
    and its Renwick Gallery
Smithsonian Institution Libraries
Smithsonian Institution Archives
Smithsonian Astrophysical Observatory
Smithsonian Center for Folklife
    and Cultural Heritage
Smithsonian Environmental Research Center
Smithsonian Photographic Services
Smithsonian Tropical Research Institute
Smithsonian Women's Committee,
    Office of Development

Smithsonian Goes Wild

Cheetah Cub

Digital photograph
National Zoo

Where can you see a regal lion from Africa and a folk art lion made from bottlecaps, an endangered Sumatran tiger and a sleek bronze leopard, a Mexican jaguar mask and sparkling cat's eye gems, as well as a host of more familiar cats, from wildcats to Felix the Cat? For those fascinated by all things feline the Smithsonian has it all. But with seventeen museums and a zoo in Washington, D.C., two museums in New York City, various research centers, and more than 137 million objects in all, the Smithsonian can be overwhelming—even for those who have the opportunity to come often. *Smithsonian Goes Wild* offers a selection of unique items from its many collections and allows you to see them as no other visitor can. In these pages you can experience highlights from the exhibits as well as see lesser-known items that are seldom on view. Here you can watch the National Zoo's cheetahs in motion and view a painting of Muhammad Ali playing cat's cradle. A catfish from the National Museum of Natural History may be swimming near "Cat's Parade" sheet music from the National Museum of American History. Curl up with kittens photographed on a military ship from the National Air and Space Museum or go wild with a panther from the Smithsonian's Tropical Research Institute in Panama. Enjoy the world's largest museum, cultural, and scientific complex without planning a trip, fighting the crowds, or leaving your pet. And return as often as you like.

Group of Cheetahs

Digital photograph
National Zoo

With all the spotted cats in their care, one might wonder—how do zoo keepers tell the cheetahs apart? Fortunately, every cheetah's tail has unique stripes, just as every person has a unique set of fingerprints. Cheetahs are the world's fastest mammals and also one of its most endangered. Visitors to the National Zoo are often amazed to catch a fleeting glimpse of them running through their vast yard. In the wild cheetahs live in open savannas and stalk hoofed animals for food. Sadly, they are often killed by farmers who consider them pests and by larger predators who consider them competition for survival. The Zoo participates in programs to save the cat from extinction.

Lion

Digital photograph
National Zoo

This magnificent lion seems to be yawning rather than roaring, but visitors to the National Zoo should not underestimate his power. Lions have strong forelegs, teeth, and jaws for tackling and killing their prey. The males, who have shaggy manes, can grow up to 10 feet long and weigh anywhere from 330 to 530 pounds. Lions live primarily in the open plains, thick brush, and dry thorn forests of Africa. In the wild they eat large animals, such as zebras and wildebeests. The Zoo's keepers feed the lions in their care "Natural Balance," a beef product, and twice weekly, beef femurs to help with their dental care.

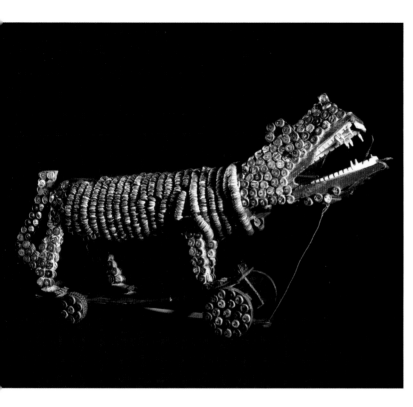

Bottlecap Lion

Completed after 1966
Unidentified artist
Carved and painted assemblage, bottlecaps,
flashcube, fiberboard, and plastic
Smithsonian American Art Museum
Gift of Herbert Waide Hemphill, Jr. and
museum purchase made possible by Ralph
Cross Johnson

Bottlecap Lion is among the treasures
in the Smithsonian American Art
Museum's folk art collection, acquired in
the 1980s from the pioneering collector
Herbert Waide Hemphill, Jr. Since their
introduction in the 1890s, bottlecaps
have become popular collectibles.
Made to resemble a large pull toy, this
mechanical feline exhibits caps from an
impressive assortment of beverages.

Figure

c.1913-1917
Fon Peoples
Porto Novo, Republic of Benin
Silver
National Museum of African Art
Museum purchase

This silver figure of a man riding a lion represents Oudji, paramount chief of Porto Novo, who reigned from 1913 to 1929. Oudji holds a plate engraved with his name and that of Charles Noufflard, French governor of Dahomey from c.1912-1913 to c.1917-1919. The figure was almost certainly commissioned by Oudji himself as a gift to Noufflard. Oudji's power to rule is expressed symbolically by his being mounted atop a lion. As ruler, Oudji controlled his kingdom's wealth, represented by the purse hanging at his side.

Lions in the Desert

c.1897-1900
Henry Ossawa Tanner
Oil on canvas mounted on plywood
Smithsonian American Art Museum
Gift of Mr. and Mrs. Norman Robbins

Regal lions rise majestically from the
sand. They are the work of Henry O.
Tanner (1859-1937), the son of an
African American minister and the
descendant of slaves. Tanner moved to
Paris in 1891, convinced that he would
never realize his artistic potential in
America, where racial discrimination
was rampant. In Europe, he won
acclaim for his work depicting African
American subjects and for canvases
based on religious themes. He inspired
an entire generation of young black
artists and is considered to be one
of the most distinguished African
American artists of the nineteenth
century.

The Great Pyramid and the Great Sphinx, from Egypt, Sinai, and Jerusalem Portfolio

1858
Francis Frith
Albumen print
National Museum of American History
Photographic History Collection

The enigmatic Sphinx, with the head of a man and the body of a lion, reclines before the Great Pyramid. Francis Frith took this majestic shot in 1858. A native of England, Frith (1822-1898) made his first tour of Egypt and Palestine in 1856-1857, where he had to develop his negatives in tombs and caves due to the oppressive heat and blinding light of the desert. During later trips to the Middle East, he visited Jerusalem, Syria, Lebanon, and Nubia. A successful businessman, he eventually established the Francis Frith Company to house and sell his own work.

Three Kittens in Toy Air Ship

n.d.
Photograph for children's book *Four Little Kittens* by Harry Whittier Frees
National Air and Space Museum Archives

Harry Whittier Frees was the author of several children's books starring posed animals. This image from *Four Little Kittens* appeared in the *New York Herald Tribune* of January 18, 1931. Only three of the four mischievous kittens are featured here. Under the headline "All aboard for Cloudland," the original text reads, "Susie and her little sister were a little nervous when they began their first ride on the transcontinental blimp express. Only the pilot appeared confident." Airships continue to fascinate people and all kinds of airship ephemera may be found in the National Air and Space Museum Archives.

Mascots aboard the *USS* **Richmond**

1924
Photographer unknown,
possibly Leslie Arnold
Photograph
National Air and Space Museum Archives
Leslie Arnold Collection

The two adorable kittens engaged in a sparing match aboard the USS *Richmond* caught the attention of several crewmen, seen in the background, as well as the interest of the photographer. The photo is found in the Leslie Arnold Collection in the National Air and Space Museum Archives. Arnold was a lieutenant in the Army Air Service in 1924 and a crew member in one of the three Army Douglas World Cruiser biplanes that made a 27,000-mile journey around the world in 175 days. Archives users may access his diary of that journey, as well as scrapbooks, photographs, and maps.

The Blue Thread

1984
Will Barnet
Oil on canvas
Smithsonian American Art Museum
Gift of Frank K. Ribelin and museum
purchase through the Luisita L. and Franz H.
Denghausen Endowment
Art © Will Barnet/Licensed by VAGA,
New York, NY

The cat in this picture fits snuggly between the mother, busy with her knitting needles and yarn, and the child, whose toy mallet is poised to strike wooden pegs. The cat rests comfortably between the two windows—motionless and wise in this warm domestic scene. Oddly, the animal is neither tempted by the yarn nor the youngster. Will Barnet (b. 1911), a painter and printmaker who taught at the Art Student's League in New York in the 1930s, experimented with abstraction but remained a figurative painter for most of his career. Many of his later works focus on the themes of human relationships and meditation.

Maya Lin

1988
Michael Katakis
Gelatin silver print
National Portrait Gallery
Gift of Michael Katakis in memory of his
father, George E. Katakis
Courtesy of Michael Katakis

As an undergraduate at Yale University, Maya Lin (b. 1959) submitted a design for a Vietnam War memorial as part of a class assignment. She later sent her untraditional concept—a V-shaped wall of black marble inscribed with the names of more than 57,000 casualties of war—to a nationwide competition. Her simple work won her the commission, and Lin's Vietnam Veterans Memorial now has a prominent place on the National Mall. Since earning fame for the memorial, Lin has made her mark with other significant public commissions. Here, she shares a private moment with her cat.

La Baronne Emile D'Erlanger

c. 1924
Romaine Brooks
Oil on canvas
Smithsonian American Art Museum
Gift of the artist

Romaine Brooks (1874-1970) painted this elegant portrait of Emile D'Erlanger. It is dominated by the artist's typical palette of blacks, whites, and grays, with warmer tones reserved for the baroness' dress and the cat's coat, which bear a striking resemblance to one another. Like his mistress, the cat has an aristocratic bearing. Even as the cage is held open by his owner's hand, the animal remains motionless, unwilling or unable to claim his freedom. Brooks, too, was a captive of sorts. Raised by a cruel mother, she sought refuge in the bohemian haunts of Europe, but could never escape the scars of her childhood.

Lady Holding a Cat

c. 1810
Katsushika Hokusai
Japanese, Edo period
Ink on paper
Freer Gallery of Art
Gift of Charles Lang Freer

A Japanese courtesan snuggles her cat in
this lovely sketch by Katsushika Hokusai.
Hokusai was the first Japanese artist to
become widely known in the West, and
his iconic block print *The Great Wave* is
one of the most recognized images in
the world. The artist was born in 1760
in Edo (d. 1849), where he produced
brilliant pictures that profoundly
influenced European and American
design and popular culture. Visitors
to the Smithsonian's Freer and Sackler
Galleries may view several of his exquisite
original works.

Key Marco Cat

15th-16th century
Southwest coast, Florida
Wood
National Museum of Natural History

The Calusa Indians settled and thrived in Marco Island's mangrove swamps centuries ago. They were accomplished artists, as evidenced by this amazing cat sculpture from about the fifteenth century, which was uncovered during an archaeological expedition in 1896. The six-inch-high wooden artifact, which appears to be part feline and part human, survived intact, possibly because it was buried deep in the muck without exposure to oxygen and other elements.

Elegance

c.1927
Heinz Warneke
Marble
Smithsonian American Art Museum
Gift of Julia Bretzman

With the arch of its body and rotation
of its delicate head, the cat is indeed
elegance personified. Heinz Warneke
(1895-1983), who was born and trained
in Germany but later immigrated to the
United States, was well known for his
animal sculptures. Among his famous
works is an elephant group for the
Philadelphia Zoo and sculptures for the
National Cathedral in Washington, D.C.

Amulet of a Goddess, Perhaps Sakhmet

c. 1075-656
 B.C.E or later
Third Intermediate Period
Possibly Saite Dynasty 26
Amulet and faience (glazed composite)
Egypt
Freer Gallery of Art
Gift of Charles Lang Freer

This ancient amulet has the body of a woman and the head of a lioness. It depicts either the Egyptian goddess Sakhmet or the goddess Bastet. Sakhmet, a lion-headed goddess, was a symbol of power and protection for the Egyptian king. Bastet was the feline-headed counterpart of Sakhmet. Because there is no inscription on the amulet, scholars are unsure of the figure's true identity. On the goddess' head is a sun disk with a cobra-like serpent, which represents the radiance of the sun god.

Black Panther

1928
Bruce Moore
Bronze
Smithsonian American Art Museum
Gift of Alice H. Moore

Sculptor Bruce Moore (1905-1980) was clearly fascinated by animals and several of his works in the Smithsonian American Art Museum's collections depict them. His artistic skill is evident in this finely cast bronze panther with its sleek lines and powerful sense of movement. Moore's drawing of bird skulls and bills and a study of chicken feet, also in the museum's collections, show his obsession with representing animal anatomy accurately.

Happy, Crazy, American Animals and a Man and Lady at My Place

1961
John Wilde
Oil on wood
Smithsonian American Art Museum
Gift of S. C. Johnson & Son, Inc.

This image lives up to the artist's last name. It is a wonderfully hectic canvas in which nature runs free indoors, a woman bares her natural self, and a man quietly observes the chaos from the back room. One wild cat plays with yarn at center, while another waits his turn in the room at left. John Wilde (1919-2006), a leader in the American surrealist movement, was famous for his fine draftsmanship, still lifes featuring skewed perspectives, and enigmatic and provocative scenes of friends and loved ones.

Jaguar Performer

Smithsonian Folklife Festival 2004
Digital photograph
Smithsonian Center for Folklife and
Cultural Heritage

This dancing jaguar was featured in an exhibit called "Nuestra Música: Music in Latino Culture" at the 2004 Smithsonian Folklife Festival. In Central and South America, the jaguar has long been a symbol of power and strength. For the Maya, jaguars facilitated communication between the world of the living and the dead and were believed to be their companions in the spiritual world. The Aztecs used the jaguar image to represent rulers or warriors. In the United States, we too use these animals as symbols of strength, elegance, and speed. Not only is jaguar the name of a luxury car, but it is also the mascot of several sports teams.

The Circus

1971
Albina Felski
Acrylic on canvas
Smithsonian American Art Museum
Gift of Herbert Waide Hemphill, Jr.
and museum purchase made possible
by Ralph Cross Johnson

Albina Felski (1916-1996) did not begin painting until 1960, but quickly developed her natural talent for brightly colored, minutely detailed canvases. This work crams every conceivable circus act into a single four-by-four-foot canvas. The lions at the bottom wait patiently in their cages, while the tigers and their trainer perform at center. A native of British Columbia, Canada, Felski spent decades working in an electronics factory in Chicago, while painting in her free time.

Around a Hole in Space
(Circus World Museum)

1973
Clarence John Laughlin
Gelatin silver print on paper mounted on
paperboard
Smithsonian American Art Museum
Transfer from the National Endowment for
the Arts

The lion in this photograph is trapped
in a decorative design, perhaps part
of an artifact at the Circus World
Museum, but the context is unclear.
Laughlin (1905-1985), a self-taught
photographer from Louisiana, focused
his lens on diverse subjects and
experimented with different styles and
techniques. He created abstractions of
architectural features and also staged
allegories using costumes and props,
creating distinctly surreal images.
Laughlin strove to communicate a
hidden reality, one not addressed by any
movement or religion.

Black Panther

1934
Alice Dinneen
Oil on canvas
Smithsonian American Art Museum
Transfer from the U.S. Department of Labor

Some of Alice Dineen's colorful works were created for the U.S. Treasury-sponsored art programs of the 1930s and 1940s. The goal of these programs was to decorate public buildings with murals and other forms of high quality art. Dineen's *Black Panther* was also a work of public art, created for the New Deal's Works Progress Administration (WPA). The sleek animal lies beneath brilliant foliage in a canvas reminiscent of the exotic jungles created by French artist Henri Rousseau.

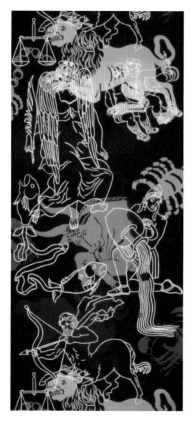

Sidewall: *Zodiac*

1942
Galena, Illinois
Designed by Marion Dorn
Produced by Bassett & Vollum, Inc.
Screen printed on paper
Cooper-Hewitt, National Design Museum
Gift of anonymous donor

Marion Dorn (1899-1964) distinguished herself in the field of interior design in England in the 1930s. Born in the United States, she married an Englishman and moved to England in 1923, where she founded her own business in London in 1934. Dorn created innovative designs that were primarily abstract, but she did not completely abandon figurative motifs. Her work often depicted animals, such as the lion, crab, and ram in this zodiac. Dorn also designed carpets for the Claridge, Savoy, and Berkeley hotels, as well as for some of the Cunard Line's ships, including the *Queen Mary.*

Tiger

1977
Felipe Archuleta
Carved and painted cottonwood, sawdust, and marbles
Smithsonian American Art Museum
Gift of David L. Davies

Acclaimed folk sculptor Felipe Archuleta (1910-1991) fashioned this tiger with carpenter's tools, nails, and glue. The open mouth, glaring eyes and bared teeth give a ferocious feel to the figure. Archuleta lived most of his life in Tesuque, New Mexico, where he worked as a carpenter, short-order cook, migrant worker, and drummer. Poor and out of work in the late 1960s, Archuleta experienced a religious awakening and began to carve wooden animals, such as this tiger. Many were based on pictures he found in children's books and natural history magazines.

Sumatran Tiger

Digital photograph
National Zoo

A powerful and agile hunter, with strong teeth and jaws, the tiger has distinctive striped fur. Tigers have been classified by scientists into nine subspecies: Bali, Java, Caspian, Sumatran, Amur (or Siberian), Indian (or Bengal), South China, Malayan, and Indo-Chinese. The first three noted are extinct. The Sumatran tiger pictured here was born and raised at the Smithsonian's National Zoo in Washington, D.C. Scientists study the Zoo's tigers in order to understand how to best conserve the tiger in its natural habitat of Sumatra's dense and humid rainforests.

Made Harmless at Last

1884
Frederich Graetz
Chromolithograph on paper
National Portrait Gallery

Theodore Roosevelt and Grover Cleveland are shown here with giant scissors, which they used to declaw and defang the Tammany tiger—a symbol of the corrupt Democratic Party. The subdued animal is slumped over in his plush chair—all his powers having been stripped. The likenesses of Roosevelt and Cleveland would have immediately been recognized by readers of *Puck*, a humor magazine, in which this cartoon first appeared in 1894.

Number 3, 1949: Tiger

1949
Jackson Pollock
Oil, enamel, metallic enamel, and cigarette
fragment on canvas mounted on fiberboard
Hirshhorn Museum and Sculpture Garden
Gift of Joseph H. Hirshhorn, 1972
©2007 The Pollock-Krasner Foundation/
Artists Rights Society (ARS), New York

One of Jackson Pollock's (1912-1956) famous poured paintings, this nonrepresentational canvas has the colors and energy of a tiger, if not the actual image of one. Pollock began to paint in this style around 1947, spreading the canvas on his studio floor and pouring, dripping, and splattering paint directly onto it from a brush or stick. Because the process of creating the painting is evident in its final form, Pollock's work has been seen as an extension of the artist's being—a record of his physical labor to create the picture, as well as a mirror into his soul.

Panthera onca (Jaguar)

2005
Color photograph
Smithsonian Tropical Research Institute

Panthera onca (jaguar) is the largest cat in the Western Hemisphere and, after the lion and tiger, the third largest cat in the world. Historically, jaguars have not been harmful to people but because their habitat is slowly disappearing, they have begun to invade ranches and prey on cattle. This jaguar was photographed in Panama, home of the Smithsonian's Tropical Research Institute (STRI). The conservation of this beautiful cat's forest domain is the focus of some of STRI's research scientists.

Jaguar Qero

A.D 1550-1800
Peru, Inca
Painted wood
National Museum of the American Indian

The National Museum of the American Indian has the newest museum building on the National Mall. Completed in 2004, its design is characterized by sweeping curves of earth-colored stone, reminding visitors of Native Americans' ties to the land. Among the 8,000 objects in its collections is this *qero* from Peru. Hand carved and hand painted, it served as a ceremonial cup in Incan rituals.

Leopard

c. 1932-1935
Paul Manship
Bronze
Smithsonian American Art Museum
Gift of the artist

Paul Manship (1885-1966) knew by the age of fifteen that he wanted to be a sculptor. By 1912, he had studied art in New York, appreciated Greek antiquity and classicism in Rome, and returned to the United States, where he won public praise for his graceful bronzes. Manship's stately leopard reveals the artist's skill in conveying not just the look but the nature of the wild cat. Poised and strong, the leopard looks as though he might spring from his pedestal. Manship embraced art deco design and created highly stylized neoclassical works. Among his most famous commissions are *Prometheus* in New York's Rockefeller Center and the gates of the Bronx and Central Park zoos.

Caracal

Digital photo
National Zoo

The caracal is a wild cat about the size of a cocker spaniel dog. It lives in semi-arid climates and is distributed across Africa, Turkey, the Arabian Peninsula, the Middle East, southern and central India, and southwestern Asia. While the body of the caracal looks like that of a domestic house cat, the tufts of black fur on its triangular ears more closely resemble the features of lynxes and jungle cats. Although it appears cute and docile in this photo, the caracal has powerful hind legs, killer claws, and strong jaws to attack and eat its prey.

Portrait of Art Goebel Holding Air Show Trophies

n.d.
Photographer unknown
Gelatin silver print
National Air and Space Museum Archives

Art Goebel, a dashing barnstormer and memorable figure in early aviation, belonged to an unusual organization known as the "13 Black Cats." These pilots specialized in stunt flying, parachute jumping, wing-walking, and other aerial feats in the early days of Hollywood. With both male and female members, the group performed upside-down plane changes, automobile-to- plane changes, and crashes with parachute drops. But Goebel's talent went far beyond such daredevil acts. In 1927, he won the Dole Race from Oakland to Honolulu. Flying the *Woolarac* in risky weather across the Pacific, Goebel made the 2,439-mile flight in 27 hours, 17 minutes, and 33 seconds and won the $25,000 prize.

Soldier with Tuba and Kitten

June 8, 1942
Rudy Arnold
Color photograph
National Air and Space Museum Archives
Rudy Arnold Photo Collection

Although Rudy Arnold (1902-1966) was primarily an aviation photographer for much of his career, some images in this extensive collection do not feature airplanes. It is not known what circumstances led to a kitten being placed in the horn of a soldier's tuba on June 8, 1942, but we can surmise that the shot was irresistible to Arnold. With his paws gripping the edge precariously and his body leaning forward, the little cat seems to be pondering how to best liberate himself from the deafening instrument.

Black Mountain Lion and Black Fox

c.1925-1930
Awa Tsireh
Watercolor, ink, and pencil on paper
Smithsonian American Art Museum
Corbin-Henderson Collection
Gift of Alice H. Rossin

Awa Tsireh was born in San Ildefonso
Pueblo, New Mexico, and became
one of the first Pueblo painters to
earn recognition in the Santa Fe Arts
community. Although many of his
paintings sold for less than a dollar,
his efforts encouraged other Native
American artists to try the watercolor
medium and market their work. In
the 1920s Tsireh received sponsorship
from a branch of the Museum of
New Mexico so he could devote all
his time to painting. In this work, a
black mountain lion and black fox are
set beneath a central sun and under a
rainbowlike design. Each animal bears a
Pueblo symbol.

Halloween Joys

c. 1910
Printed postcard
National Air and Space Museum Archives
Krainick Ballooning Collection

The Krainik Ballooning Collection in the archives of the National Air and Space Museum contains memorabilia related to ballooning from the nineteenth and twentieth centuries—stereoscopic photographs, postcards, trade cards, photographs, and prints. Among its highlights are stereoscopic images of T.S. Lowe's surveillance balloons during the Civil War and views of balloons during the Boer War, Russo-Japanese War, and World War I. This whimsical postcard is also part of the collection. Adventurous black cats are seen flying jack-o-lantern balloons for Halloween.

J. Kathleen White to Ellen H. Johnson

September 1, 1968
Handwritten letter
Archives of American Art
Ellen Hulda Johnson Papers

This 1986 letter from writer J. Kathleen White (b. 1952) to art educator Ellen Hulda Johnson (1910-1992) features a cat that White says was composed on "an incredible device" called a computer! Ellen Johnson was a dynamic force in the contemporary art scene for several decades of the twentieth century. She was the first to recognize the talents of such artists as Claes Oldenburg, Larry Poons, and Bruce Nauman. She was also a popular and influential teacher at her alma mater, Oberlin College. Her papers may be found at the Smithsonian's Archives of American Art.

Matchsafe with cover of The Sportsman *magazine*

1899-1900
Unidentified makers mark (W.N.)
Chester, England
Silver, enamel
Cooper-Hewitt, National Design Museum
Gift of Stephen W. Brener and
Carol B. Brener

A kangaroo and lion play cricket in
this fancy matchbox that is also an
advertisement for "Cricket News."
Fanciful matchsafes such as this one
were used in the late nineteenth and
early twentieth centuries to keep
matches dry but often served to promote
various products as well. The Cooper-
Hewitt, National Design Museum has an
extraordinary collection of matchsafes in
a wide range of designs.

Three Hybrids

1995
Stephan Balkenhol
Synthetic polymer on wood
Hirshhorn Museum and Sculpture Garden
Joseph H. Hirshhorn Bequest Fund, 1995
Courtesy Gladstone Gallery, New York, NY

Born in Germany in 1957, Stephan
Balkenhol is known for his carved
figures. Whimsical in nature, the works
incorporate the everyday mundane
qualities of men and women with the
unexpected. Here, perfectly ordinary
male figures in casual pose have the
heads of animals. The central slouching
figure is a rather un-regal lion. All the
figures stand on elevated pedestals in
the manner of classical statues.

"Greetings from New South Wales"

1900
H. Phillips
Taronga Zoological Park
Katoomba, New South Wales
National Zoological Park Collections
Smithsonian Institution Libraries

The National Zoological Park branch of the Smithsonian Institution Libraries has a collection of historic pamphlets and guidebooks from zoos in more than thirty states and forty countries. When viewed together, they trace the history of the modern zoo, from recreation areas, amusements parks, and showcases for "oddities," to serious institutions that study, care for, and conserve diverse species.

Four Women with a Cat

c. 1865
Unknown photographer
Tintype
National Museum of American History
Photographic History Collection

Formal studio portraits like this one
were common in the late 1800s, as
was the process of printing them as
a tintype. The tintype process was
much faster and easier than the earlier
glass-plated ambrotype and silver-
plated daguerreotype. The first form
of "instant photo," the tintype was
a negative image that appeared as a
positive due to the lacquered black
base on which it rested. Because the
image was on durable metal, it could be
trimmed and put in lockets and cases.
While the occasion for this tintype
and the identities of the women are
unknown, it is clear that the cat is of
utmost importance as it holds center
stage in the composition.

Cat's Cradle

1981
Henry C. Casselli, Jr.
Oil on canvas
National Portrait Gallery
Gift of the Sig Rogich Family Trust
©2002 Henry Casselli

Three-time heavyweight boxing champion Muhammad Ali is depicted in this 1981 canvas extending the hands that made him "The Greatest" in the string game cat's cradle. The winner of Sonny Liston's title and inspiration for the movie *Rocky,* Ali suffered many setbacks after coming out of retirement in the 1980s to challenge Larry Holmes. However, his loss in that fight and subsequent diagnosis of Parkinson 's disease did not totally end his career. A much loved and active public figure, Ali, a convert to Islam, founded the Muhammad Ali Center to promote peace, social responsibility, and respect.

Int'l Surface No. 1

1960
Stuart Davis
Oil on canvas
Smithsonian American Art Museum
Gift of S.C. Johnson & Son, Inc.
Art ©Estate of Stuart Davis/Licensed by
VAGA, New York, NY

Stuart Davis (1894-1964) was greatly
influenced by European modernism,
and by 1915 he was experimenting with
cubist abstraction, a style that defined
his painting for decades, including this
later work, *Int'l Surface No. 1*. Jazz
was also an important influence on the
artist. He introduced the rhythms of
the music in his collages and canvases,
played with geometry and space, and
juxtaposed themes of American popular
culture, such as billboards, cigarette
packs, and simple words. Here, "cat"
and "juice" are featured, which double
as musical slang.

"Treat 'Em Rough, Join the Tanks"

Poster, four-color print on paper
National Museum of American History
Division of Military History and Diplomacy

Intended to evoke strong emotion—fear of the enemy, fear of war—as well as pride and patriotism, posters produced for World Wars I and II often had bold graphics and simple slogans. Many of those in the collection of the National Museum of American History encourage citizens to help with the war effort, ask them to endure personal sacrifice on behalf of freedom, and urge rationing and conservation of everyday items. This frightening black cat—a symbol of both power and superstition—surely persuaded a few people to enlist.

Poster Calendar

1897
Edward Penfield
Color lithograph
National Portrait Gallery

As a staff illustrator for *Harper's Weekly*, Edward Penfield (1866-1925) emerged as a talented young artist. The shy, retiring New Yorker ultimately produced bold graphic images for which he was credited as the "originator of the poster in America." Many examples of his graphic work may be viewed at the National Portrait Gallery and, interestingly, several of his advertising images —calendars, magazine covers— feature faithful cats. Penfield also served as art director, graphic designer, writer, painter, educator, and mentor throughout his long art career.

"Belgium Shall Be Free Again"

Postmark November 1943
Patriotic cover
Unknown publisher
Scott Catalogue USA: 905
Paper, ink, adhesive
National Postal Museum

Patriotic covers from the United States and other nations are collected by the National Postal Museum. During the Second World War, such illustrated stationery revealed strong emotions of people on all sides of the conflict. This cover, postmarked November 1, 1943, pictures Belgium encircled by a Nazi chain. The Belgian lion at right holds a sword aloft and touches the Shield of Victory. With the slogan "Belgium Shall Be Free Again," the cover's purpose was to rally Americans to join the war effort and also served to boost the morale of those already in the fray.

Man with the Cat
(Henry Sturgis Drinker)

1898
Cecilia Beaux
Oil on canvas
Smithsonian American Art Museum
Bequest of Henry Ward Ranger through
the National Academy of Design

The aristocratic Mr. Drinker, the artist's
brother-in-law as well as a railroad
executive who later became president
of Lehigh University, is bathed in light.
His distinctive whiskers and intense gaze
convey an authority and strength of
character that a man of such influence
in the 1890s surely possessed. But the
furry cat nestled in his lap suggests a
softer side. Cecilia Beaux (1855-1942),
an independent woman who rivaled the
great male portraitists of her time, may
have enjoyed bringing these diverse sit-
ters together in a single canvas.

Glyptothorax nelsoni
(Catfish)

2004
Digital photograph
National Museum of Natural History
Division of Fishes

Glyptothorax is a genus of sucker catfishes, or sisorid catfishes (Sisoridae). There are more than sixty-five species of *Glypotothorax*, one of which, *Glyptothorax nelsoni*, is pictured here. These fish have a wide geographic distribution. They live in fast-flowing streams and use the "suckers" on their underside to attach to rocks to protect them from being washed away by strong currents.

Cat's Eye Gems

Color photograph
National Museum of Natural History
National Gem Collection

Those who know and love cats are captivated by their eyes, which have a narrow pupil within a luminous iris. Many minerals can be cut as "cat's eye gems," so named because of the narrow bright band of light in a shimmering background. The band of light seems to glide across the surface of these extraordinary examples, which are, clockwise from top center: 171.6 carat cat's eye chrysoberyl from Sri Lanka; green elbaite gem, 53.2 carats from Brazil; pink elbaite gem, 17.5 carats from California; teal-colored elbaite gem, 65.5 carats from Brazil; two scapolite gems from Burma – white 29.9 carats and purple 3.3 carats; and golden beryl, 43.5 carats from Madagascar.

Giant Lions-Paw Shell

Color photograph
National Museum of Natural History
Division of Mollusks

This giant lions-paw shell is part of the collection of the Division of Mollusks at the Smithsonian's National Museum of Natural History. The second largest phyllum after Anthropoda, Mollusca includes more than 100,000 species, including snails, clams, squids, and octopuses. Many mollusks have hard shells to protect their soft bodies. Biologists study specimens in the Smithsonian collection of mollusks to discover how these animals live and adapt.

Cat with Mouse

c. 1870
Kawanabe Kyosai
Woodblock print; ink and color on paper
Arthur M. Sackler Gallery
Robert O. Muller Collection

This humorous image of a cat toying casually with a struggling mouse is the work of Japanese artist Kawanabe Kyosai. Not much is known about Kyosai's personal history but he is said to have lived a life of lively excess and often executed his wonderful images while under the influence of sake (rice wine). Kyosai was a master of ink and brush painting technique, several examples of which may be viewed at the Freer and Sackler Galleries.

"Felix the Wonderful Cat"

1928
Sheet music
Sam DeVincent Collection of Illustrated American
Sheet Music
Archives Center
National Museum of American History
Permission to use image provided courtesy of Don
Oriolo and FTCP, Inc. © 2007 and ™ Felix the Cat
Productions, Inc.

This mischievous cat is the figure we know and love from the classic cartoon series "Felix the Cat." Created by New Jersey cartoonist Otto Messmer, Felix debuted in a short film called *Feline Follies* in the early 1900s and then appeared in print in 250 newspapers worldwide. His fellow characters in the popular TV series "Felix the Cat"—Poindexter, the Professor, Rock Bottom, and Vavoom, as well as his Bag of Tricks—were actually the brainchild of Messmer's protégé Joe Oriolo. This sheet music from the Archives Center at the National Museum of American History shows the loveable cat at his best.

Tiger

18th century
Katayama Yokoku
Japanese, Edo period, 1762-1803
Nagasaki school, Japan
Hanging scroll, ink on paper
Freer Gallery of Art
Museum purchase

This tiger scroll is the work of painter Katayama Yokoku (1760-1801). Scroll painting originated in China and was used to teach Buddhist moral lessons. The scrolls were later used to display and maintain works of pictorial art. Edo scrolls are somewhat shorter than their Chinese predecessors and use a more subdued palette to achieve a refined yet powerful effect.

Lionkeepers

After 1870
Antoin Sevruguin
Silver print
Freer Gallery of Art and Arthur M. Sackler Gallery Archives
Myron Bement Smith Collection, Gift of Katharine Dennis Smith

Antoin Sevruguin (1830s-1933) was an official photographer of the Imperial Court of Iran and had a successful commercial photography studio in Tehran from the 1880s to 1930s. During that time, he took images of Iranian society, public events, and daily life such as these lion keepers and their sleepy charge. Two of them are armed with sticks while the man at left keeps his eyes trained on the great cat, just in case he makes a sudden move.

1900
Composed by Lee Johnson
Sheet music
Published by Lee Johnson & Co., San Francisco
Sam DeVincent Collection of Illustrated American Sheet Music
Archives Center, National Museum of American History

Lee Johnson was a composer of vaudeville music for minstrel shows around the turn of the twentieth century. Among his titles are "My Honolulu Lady" and "Parson Johnson's Chicken Brigade." This "Cats' Parade" sheet music has an amusing cover. A group of felines gathers on a moonlit rooftop to conduct a musical midnight revel, much to the displeasure of the unhappy onlooker at left.

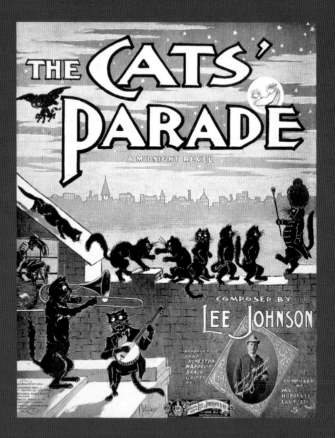

1960
Sheet music from the Broadway musical
Wildcat
Score by Cy Coleman and Carolyn Leigh
Sam DeVincent Collection of Illustrated
American Sheet Music
Archives Center, National Museum of
American History
Image of Lucille Ball used with permission of
Desilu, too, LLC

Lucille Ball of *I Love Lucy* fame starred in
the Broadway musical *Wildcat,* a story
about a woman who must abandon
her wild, competitive nature to win
the man of her dreams. Zany and
enjoyable, Lucy was a hit in the show,
but the production closed after only
162 performances. *Wildcat* may now
be heard on CD and the sheet music for
one of its songs, "One Day We Dance,"
may be viewed in the Sam DeVincent
Collection of Illustrated American Sheet
Music at the Archives Center in the
National Museum of American History.

Supremacy

1887
Frederick Stuart Church
Oil on canvas
Smithsonian American Art Museum
Gift of John Gellatly

Not to be confused with Hudson River
School artist Frederic Edwin Church,
Frederick Stuart Church (1842-1924)
was born in Grand Rapids, Michigan,
and moved to New York to pursue
a career as an artist. Animals in
Church's paintings often have human
characteristics and interact easily with
people. In *Supremacy* the woman who
casually embraces the lion's glorious
mane seems to share supremacy with
the king of all animals. Church used
real animals as models for his picture,
visiting the Central Park Zoo, as well as
the headquarters of Barnum & Bailey
Circus.

William Zorach

1936
Aline Fruhauf
Ink, pencil, and gouache on paper
National Portrait Gallery
Gift of Erwin Vollmer

American sculptor William Zorach
(1887-1997) is seen carving an elegant
cat in this wonderful ink sketch by
Aline Fruhauf. Zorach was born in
Lithuania but immigrated to the United
States at the age of four. He studied at
the Cleveland School of Art, National
Academy of Design in New York, and
traveled to Paris before settling in New
York City. Although his formal training
was not in sculpture, his personal style
characterized by simple and solid forms
made him one of the foremost sculptors
of his day.

Credits

Smithsonian accession numbers are followed by names of the photographers, when known.

p. 2   96-325
p. 3   4652-15 by Jessie Cohen
p. 5   20050131-222 by Jessie Cohen
p. 6   20050908-156 by Jessie Cohen
p. 8   4652-15 by Jessie Cohen
p. 9   1988.74.17
p. 11 95-9-1
p. 13 1983.95.184
p. 14 71.009.16
p. 15 NASM-9A02173-P
p. 17 NASM-9A01944
p. 19 1966.72
p. 20 S/NPG.91.110
p. 22 1968.18.5
p. 23 F1904.256
p. 24 77-7431 by Victor Krantz
p. 25 1972-171
p. 26 F1907.30
p. 27 1993.69
p. 28 1969.47.47
p. 29 2004-35008 by Richard Strauss
p. 30 1986.65.108
p. 31 1983.63.847

p. 32 1964.1.89
p. 33 1967-49-1-a by Ken Pelka
p. 34 1992.37.2A-B
p. 35 4S148
p. 36 NPG.96.116
p. 37 72.235
p. 38 2005-1887 by Marcos Guerra
p. 39 T105860
p. 40 1965.16.28
p. 41 1691-50
p. 42 82-8687-P
p. 43 NASM-XRA-1551-P
p. 44 1979.144.48
p. 47 NASM-7A47282-P
p. 48 5876
p. 49 1982-23-40 by Matt Flynn
p. 50 95.19.A-G
p. 52 sil24-001-01
p. 53 187
p. 55 NPG.2002.2
p. 56 1969.47.55
p. 57 2004-24874 by Joe Goulait
p. 58 NPG.84.186
p. 59 2002.2035.295
p. 60 1952.10.1

p. 61 20050426-USNM-205611 by Sarah J. Raredon
p. 62 95-40606
p. 63 2003-12114 by John Steiner
p. 64 S2003.8.493
p. 65 96-325
p. 66 F1977.23
p. 67 A0781
p. 68 96-3250
p. 69 AC0300-0000066
p. 70 1929.6.17
p. 71 NPG.83.47.A

Cover: *Sumatran Tiger*
digital photograph
National Zoo

"Felix the Wonderful Cat"
1928
Sheet music
Sam DeVincent Collection of Illustrated American Sheet Music
Archives Center
National Museum of American History
Permission to use image provided courtesy of Don Oriolo and FTCP, Inc. © 2007 and ™ Felix the Cat Productions, Inc.